Illustrations credits:
Archivio White Star/Marcello Bertinetti:
Cover, back cover, 7, 8 top, 9, 12-13, 14-15, 19, 23, 24-25, 26-27, 42-43, 49 top, 50, 51, 56, 59, 67, 71, 72-73, 74-75, 85, 91, 92, 93.
Archivio White Star/Carlo De Fabianis:
8 bottom, 20, 28, 37, 40, 45, 46, 48, 54, 55, 64-65, 69, 78 top right, 87 bottom, 88.
Archivio White Star/Angela White Bertinetti:
6, 16, 22, 36, 38, 39, 41, 44, 47, 57 top, 58, 60 bottom, 62-63, 66, 87 top, 89.
Doug Armand/Tony Stone-Franca Speranza:
35.
Yann Arthus Bertrand/Overseas:
90.
B. Bruchi/Panda Photo:
60 top.
Ciuffardi/Focus Team:
33.
Anne Conway:
17, 49 bottom, 52-53, 57 bottom, 70, 82-83, 94-95.
Marco Cristofori/SIE:
4.
Damm/Zefa:
29, 76-77.
Ary Diesendruck/Tony Stone-Franca Speranza:
84.
Cesare Gerolimetto:
18, 32, 61, 80, 81.
M. Gunther/Bios-Panda Photo:
2-3, 34.
Richard Passmore/Tony Stone-Franca Speranza:
78 left.
Streich an/Zefa:
30-31, 79.
Angelo Tondini/Focus Team:
10, 86.
Bob Zola/Overseas:
11, 21, 78 bottom right.
Kord/Zefa:
68.

Translation:
Dick Reville

Printed and bound in Singapore.

First published in English in 1991 by
Tiger Books International PLC,
London.
ISBN 1-85501-105-0

INSIDE PARIS

TEXT
SIMONA TARCHETTI

DESIGN
PATRIZIA BALOCCO

TIGER BOOKS INTERNATIONAL

2-3 Panoramic view of the city. On the left the Tour Saint-Jacques, and on the right the Hôtel de Ville.

4 The Luxor Obelisk rises majestically from the Place de la Concorde.

6 Darkness falls on the Jardins des Tuileries, the Place de la Concorde and the Arc de Triomphe.

7 Panoramic view of the city from the top of Arc de Triomphe. In the background, the white silhouette of the Sacré-Coeur Basilica.

"Paris is everything you could want it to be", wrote Frederic Chopin. It is like an enormous open-air market in which all that is joyful, intelligent and beautiful is on display: art, architecture, museums, books, restaurants and shows.

Like other multi-faceted and labyrinthine cities, Paris cannot merely be visited: it has to be stormed and possessed with enthusiasm and passion. Follow your instincts and forget other people's advice. But do not be in too much of a hurry, either. This metropolis does not induce the breathlessness of New York or London but clings to its memories and always gives you a second and a third chance.

"If you had the luck to live in Paris in your youth, afterwards no matter where you spend the rest of life it stays with you because Paris is a movable feast". Thus wrote the novelist and adventurer Ernest Hemingway, capturing the most fascinating characteristic of this memorable city: the ability to stick in the mind complete with its colours, its sounds, and its smells.

Paris, like all imperial cities, intimidates those who come to pay it homage: it seems designed to provoke envy and amazement in anyone who observes its grandeur, its historically rich monuments and continual resurfacing of the past which is capable of merging imperceptibly into the present and into its own impressive future.

At this point, a brief historical digression might be useful in order to learn about the birth and development of this city which everybody dreams of visiting at least once in his life. It was probably founded by the Parisii, a Celto-Gallic tribe who settled on the hill on the left bank of the Seine overlooking the Ile de la Cité. They were fishermen, quite unlike the warlike stereotype embodied by Astérix, who has almost become a national symbol. In fact, the Romans, under the command of Labienus met little resistance when they took control of the region and founded Lutetia (Paris). Following attacks by barbaric hordes, the inhabitants of Paris and the Roman conquerors again pulled back on to the Ile de la Cité and it was left to the Merovingian Franks under Clovis to make the city the capital of their little barbarian kingdom.

Paris remained rather isolated from the great European events until 987, when the founder of the Capetian dynasty, Hugues Capet, settled there and made it the political and economic capital of France.

The Middle Ages saw the development of the city from a commercial and mercantile point of view and, indeed, it was the income from duties which financed the construction of the imposing Gothic cathedral of Notre-Dame and the fortress of the Louvre. The merchants proved to be the backbone of the town again in 1356 when they even formed a sort of civic dictatorship.

The 14th century was as devastating for Paris as it was for the rest of France. The plague and the Hundred Years' War reduced the nation to rubble. The following century was also extremely dramatic. The Duke of Orleans was assassinated in Paris and it was this which set off the bloody conflict between the Burgundians and the Armagnacs which lasted 12 years and only ended with the arrival of the English in 1420. At the end of the

8 top The Avenue des Champs Elysées is surely the most famous and the most characteristic avenue in the city. Lined with shops, theatres and cafés, it is exceptionally lively at all hours of the day and night.

8 bottom In the "brasseries", typical bar-restaurants of Paris, one can try the various gastronomic specialities of the city.

occupation by forces from across the Channel, the city experienced a wonderful renaissance which was ruined by devastating religious wars that caused 15,000 deaths in the city of Paris alone.
The magnificent reawakening of the city came about conclusively under Henry IV who was a popular sovereign and a lover of life. It was he who put such strenuous efforts into the architectural renewal of the city and ordered the construction of the Place des Vosges and Place Dauphine, the famous Quai de l'Arsenal, Quai de l'Horloge and Quai des Orfèvres as well as the oldest bridge still standing in the city, the Pont Neuf. The year 1600 marked the beginning of the great epoch of the aristocracy, culminating in the deeds of the Sun King (Louis XIV) and concluding in the tragic Revolution of 1789.
With Napoleon, Paris once more rose to the rank of Imperial capital and centre of Europe. The Arc de Triomphe, the Austerlitz Column, and the 12 great arteries forming the Etoile complex were added, and Paris became a laboratory of new social developments. It was the first city to witness the explosion of popular revenge and the assertion of the bourgeois revolution. It was from fear of such insurrections that Napoleon III gave Baron Haussmann the job of eliminating the smaller streets and alleyways and replacing them with immense boulevards.
Towards the end of the 19th century, Paris reached the apex of its cultural brilliance: artists, writers and revolutionaries fused creative tensions and rebellious impulses together in a swirling melting-pot. Picasso, Modigliani, Gertrude Stein, Ernest

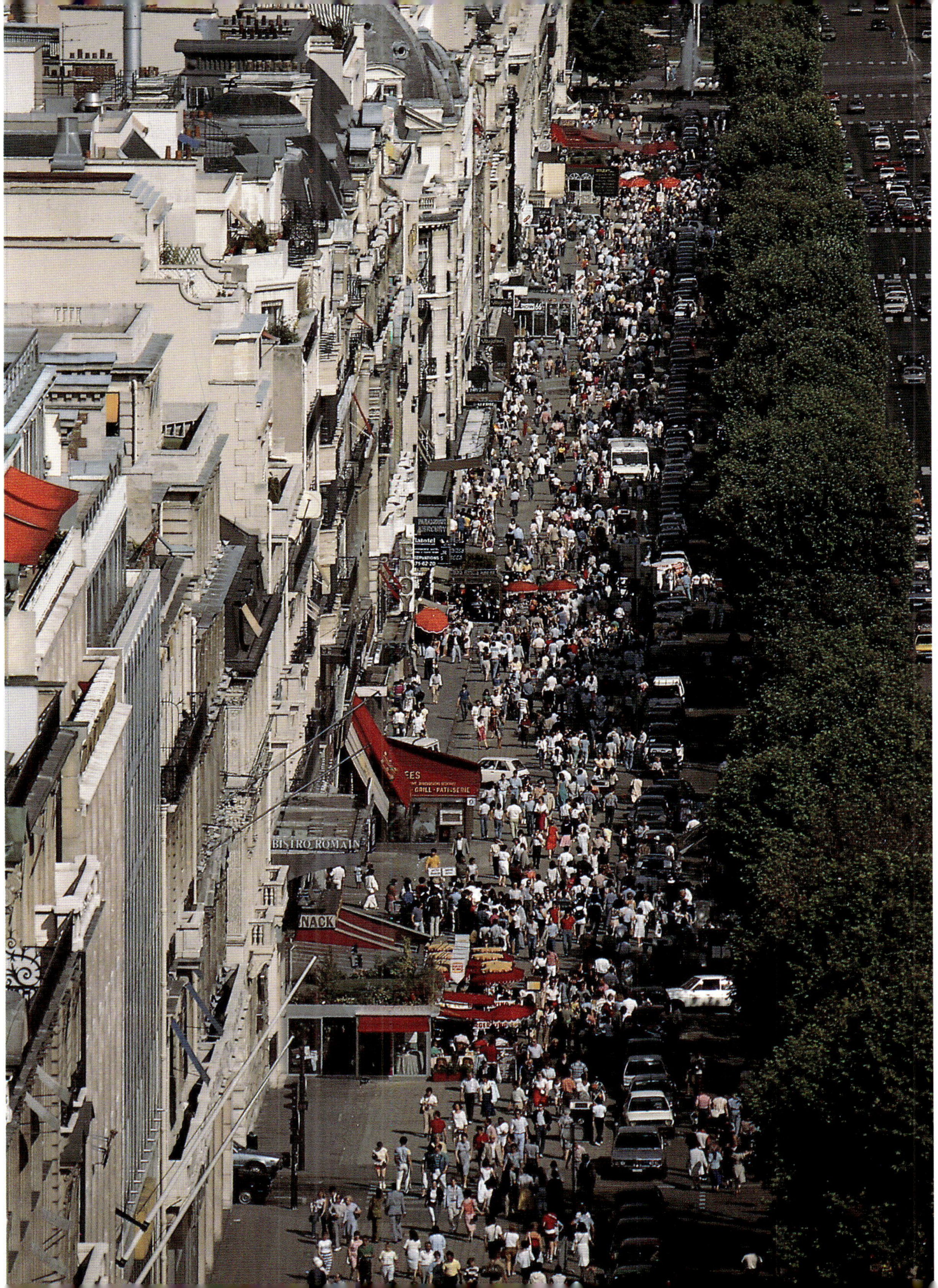

9 The imperial magnificence of the Champs Elysées: over a mile of national prestige from the Place de la Concorde to the Arc de Triomphe.

D·O·M·SVB·INVOC·S·M·MAGDALENAE

10 "La Madeleine" is situated in one of the most famous shopping areas of Paris. Originally, it was built as a temple to honour the Napoleonic soldiers of the Grande Armée, but in 1814 it became a church.

11 The Place de la Concorde was designed in the 18th century by the famous architect Gabriel. Infamous during the French Revolution, it witnessed more than 1000 executions, including those of Louis XVI and Marie Antoinette.

12-13 The Rue du Rivoli, nearly 2 miles long, has many 19th-century buildings. Along this road there are many large stores.

Hemingway, Scott Fitzgerald and Stravinsky all congregated in the city in the earlier part of this century. Soon afterwards the "Ville Lumière" handed over its palm as world capital to New York, but it continued just the same to feed its revolutionary myth with the existentialist protest of Jean Paul Sartre, the songs of Juliet Greco, and the events of 1968.
Today Paris still throws down the gauntlet. The Beaubourg cultural centre and the revival of avant-garde culture and architecture prove the vitality of a splendid synthesis between past and present in the city. This it achieves without renouncing any of its grand and terrible past and while preparing and thinking up innumerable plans and daring hypotheses for the future.
But does Paris still exist? The question is not an idle one, above all for the 12 million inhabitants who are ever more forcibly pushed towards an immense, confusing "banlieu", the suburban areas from which the metropolitan emigrants pour into the city every day. To partly resolve this demographic problem, the French government has tried the solution of satellite cities and the results are beginning to make themselves felt. One Frenchman in six lives in these outlying centres, and even though it may seem paradoxical, this fact clearly explains the function Paris has as central point for the whole of the rest of the country. Fashion, the economy and politics are shaped in this somewhat polluted but still extremely vital heart. There are no rival cities. Though Rome fears Milan and New York competes with Los Angeles, Paris commands France in everything.

SHELL
ANDRE
C&A
C&A
Julie Ambre
ACHAT
VENTE
BAR

SAMAR
RONUPTIA

14-15 View of the city: Notre-Dame can be clearly identified as well as the Hôtel de Ville, part of which was built in the neo-Renaissance style in the late 19th century.

16 Detail from the gate of the Grand Palais, which is just off the Champs Elysées.

17 The Eiffel Tower and, in the foreground one of the ornamental statues of the Palais de Chaillot.

18-19 The Opéra, designed by Charles Garnier and opened in 1875, is magnificently ornate. A false ceiling was painted by Chagall in the auditorium, and the building is also famous for the extensive use of marble in every hue.

Paris is an obligatory port-of-call for more than 5 million tourists each year who have come to see and be informed. The sightseeing tour begins: the Eiffel Tower, the Panthéon, the Louvre, Nôtre-Dame, Les Invalides . . . and a short distance away await the Champs Elysées and St Germain des Prés. Millions of shoes are worn out in the elliptical area that has its centre point in the Ile de la Cité and extends from Ile Saint Louis to the Champs-de-Mars, from the Opéra to Sainte Geneviève and on as far as Montmartre. This is the more ichnographic Paris which shows us bridges and quais, squares and designer shopping, night-life and history.
If, however, we look beyond these famous symbols, we find the city inhabited by the real Parisians. Give the monuments their due, but it is equally important to experience getting lost between Belleville and the Père-Lachaise, Faubourg St-Antoine and Gobelins. Here we are in the realm of concrete, of architectural challenges: steel and glass to satisfy the appetites of business and commerce and of a population that is growing out of all proportion and moving ever further from the centre. All things considered, this Paris which is so large and unrestrainable still manages to master itself by splitting up into many small cities each trying desperately to retain a provincial air. Not even the depersonalizing division into arrondissements has managed to destroy this process. Its inhabitants know the numbers of the arrondissements by heart but they will always talk of Montmartre, Temple and Menilmontant. The Parisian quartiers, despite the mounting invasion of offices, maintain their own characteristics and originality: thus the Latin Quarter

ACADEMIE NATIONALE DE MUSIQUE

20 The Austerlitz column in Place Vendôme. This elegant square is a superb example of late 17th-century French architecture.

21 The Colonne de Juillet is surmounted by this statue representing liberty in the Place de la Bastille. It commemorates Parisians who died in disturbances in 1830 and 1848.

continues after centuries to house an intellectual and university population, Saint Germain des Prés remains the mecca of the antiques trade and Montmartre still seems to want to defend the old Parisians who meet to play cards in the bistros, shop in the old grocery shops and play "boules" in the smog. The Seine winds its way through all these identities. The best vehicle from which to capture the city's paradoxes, changes of colour and atmosphere are the bateaux-mouches which ply up and down the river. The Seine runs for miles, sometimes almost slow and stagnant, sometimes rapid, attracted and repelled by the most diverse topography, past banks occupied by cranes or industrial buildings, past weeping willows, past little ports, restaurants and second-hand book stalls. The Seine is probably the best starting point for a visit around the city: grandiose and intimate at the same time the Seine is the real heart of Paris. A stroll along the river banks or "quais", especially early in the morning or late in the afternoon when the city is bathed in an alluring light of the most subtle tones, gives us the chance to leave the traffic and the neuroses which assault the streets and inhabitants of this global village. Dusk signals the beginning of another piece of Parisian magic: the city offers an ever-exuberant night-life.

The most inveterate male chauvinism can be satisfied in the Pigalle quartier. The Moulin Rouge, despite everything and everyone, continues to present the most brilliant variety shows in Europe. At the Michou, too, the "artists" display a certain talent. The music halls that launched Fernandel, Chevalier and Josephine Baker cannot be forgotten, either: we are talking

about the Folies-Bergères, the Casino de Paris and the Crazy Horse Saloon. The latter was developed around the most modern choreographic ideas and presents girls dressed only in points of light. Other interesting clubs crowded along the Rive-Gauche put on delightful offerings of satire and fun. We could cite L'Alcazar and the Paradis Latin, but the whole area deserves exploration. For "dancers", Paris offers a whole series of discothèques in the New York style. And the best way to root them out ? By chance, the half-given hint, things overheard in a bar.

Even the most ardent jazz freak will find some real paradises in the Latin Quarter. This is the realm of the "caves" (cellars), once the refuge of existentialists looking for relaxation after exhausting meetings. Those who prefer "serious" entertainment can rejoice at the rebirth of the Opéra where international and French celebrities have returned to sing in innovative recitals which get favourable comments from even the most discerning critics.

For those with a good knowledge of French, the whole world of French theatre is opened up, from the classical Comédie Francaise to fringe improvisations or the little shows of the chansonniers in one of the many café-theâtres which can be found in the Marais or Montparnasse areas. We really cannot forget that Paris has for centuries been a central point of reference for much of the artistic and cultural world and this has created a special brand of narcissism. Here intellectual satisfaction is lacking: you only have to head towards the post-modern galleries of the Bastille, centre of the French multimedia avant-garde, or cross the threshold of the incredible Georges Pompidou Centre where you can read, listen to records, watch films and learn foreign languages. Similary, you can pay a visit to the new temples of modern culture, the glass pyramid of the Louvre, the skyscrapers of the Défense and the "Triumphal Arch of Man". Grandeur and the idea of Utopia are on fertile ground here as the city has never abandoned its historical role as the cradle of the world of the future.

22 Paris has a wealth of ancient buildings, monuments and historic sites.

23 The Sainte-Chapelle, on the Ile de la Cité, is a fine example of Gothic architecture, and was consecrated in 1248 by order of King Louis IX (St. Louis). Its stained glass windows depict more than 1000 scenes from the Bible.

24-25 The Jardins des Tuileries were designed by the architect Le Notre in the 17th century.

26-27 The Cathedral of Notre-Dame is considered to be the most important place of worship in the entire country. A masterpiece of Gothic architecture, it is one of the oldest cathedrals in France.

28 The façade of Notre-Dame is dominated by a splendid rose-window, surrounded by large mullioned windows.

29 Notre-Dame's flying buttresses, decorated pinnacles and spires are characteristic of the Gothic style of the 13th century.

30-31 The Louvre and the Glass Pyramid: past and future come face to face.

32 Created and expanded over seven centuries, the Louvre contains works of art such as the Mona Lisa and the Venus de Milo. One week would probably not be enough to appreciate all that this wonderful treasure-house has to offer.

33 The Glass Pyramid of the Louvre covers the main entrance. Its architect was I.M. Pei, who is of Chinese-American origin.

34 The Cité des Sciences et de l'Industrie, near the Maison de la Villette, was opened in 1986 and incorporates many high-tech features. It is a massive structure, attracting thousands of visitors who come to marvel at the Planetarium, the exhibitions and, outside, the Géode, a huge globe of shining steel.

35 The Musée d'Orsay, inaugurated in December 1986, is located on the Quai Anatole France inside the Gare d'Orsay. Recently re-built by the Italian architect Gae Aulenti, it contains important Impressionist works of art.

36 The lovely Pont Mirabeau, an iron construction dating back to the end of the last century, was praised by Apollinaire.

37 A group of equestrian statues decorate the façade of the Grand Palais, built for the World Exhibition of 1900.

38-39 Scenes in the "Quartier Latin", a maze of picturesque old streets.

Paris is a busy and compulsive city, yet it conceals a secret vice of laziness and possesses a coveted and often unattainable tranquillity. You can feel this longing in the air. All Parisians secretly cultivate a penchant for langour which expresses itself in the numerous "détente-clubs". These are oases of psycho-physical relaxation where, between seaweed baths and courses of sensory isolation, you can regain the inner equilibrium for the return to the struggle in the metropolitan jungle. Then again, Paris houses the infernal circle in which the greedy (here cheerfully re-baptized as "gourmets") are ensnared. In reality, even though the capital has succeeded in imposing itself on every aspect of French life, it has not managed to create its own gastronomy. Nevertheless, it is the centre of what best expresses the taste of the five continents. The capriciousness and richness of its cuisine bring together everything capable of stimulating the appetite. Any table in Paris, from those in luxury hotels to the small bistros, will give you the same conviction: that you did not sit there just by chance or to satisfy some whim. No, the fish is always fresh and it is a crime not to taste the oysters that wink at you from every street corner. Abandon any intention of dieting and resign yourself, even if you are not dedicated to the cult of eating. For in Paris you will discover new sensations and maybe glean some secret to use at home.
After satiating the mind and body, Paris knows how to follow this up with the dizzy pleasures of shopping. It is all an invitation to squander. There are even shops specialising in welcoming foreign customers with beaming, multi-lingual hostesses to

URANT LE LATIN
Kronenbourg
LE LATIN
ENTRÉES
GRILL
Spécialités

PETROSSIAN PARIS

40-41 French cuisine and specialities have earned a world-wide reputation that is totally justified.

42 A breathtaking view of the Galeries Lafayette, which is on the Boulevard Haussmann.

43 Paris reflected in the elegant shop windows; the boutiques of the city-centre are famous for their exclusive designs.

guide you where you want to go. The names? Galeries Lafayette, Au Printemps, la Samaritaine with its superb panoramic terrace and FNAC which offers the largest selection of books and records in town. Do not forget the drugstores, all-French versions of American pharmacies and teetotal bars. Paris is a real paradise for both the ingenuous and the sophisticated hunter, the expert or the amateur on antiques. At any level the sifting takes place principally in the elegant shops of the sixth or seventh arrondissements, or in the little second-hand markets in the suburbs, like the famous Marché aux Puces, which extends from Saint-Ouen to the Porte de Clignancourt. It is actually a group of smaller markets all waiting to be seen and discovered: Vernaison, with its musical instruments, old toys and lead soldiers, or Biron with its antiques at acceptable prices. Then again there is Malik where mostly young people come for the incredible assortment of belle époque clothes and strange objects in American 1950s style. The experts can venture forth, before dawn, in search of that missing piece, to Paul Bert or to Jules Valles who sell art nouveau rarities and lamps, dolls and authentic military bric-a-brac. A chapter apart are the "bouquinistes", the second-hand booksellers who congregate along the Seine, especially Place Saint Michel and the Pont des Arts. Here you can find magazines and periodicals from before and after the war, and be overwhelmed with advice and chatter by French lovers of this intellectual and cliquish pastime.

Christian Dior
CARITA
ULTIMA II
ULTIMA II
CLARINS
Bienvenue à Paris
BALENCIAGA

unanym
georgesrech

van Laack
van Laack
Solde

44 *The daily ritual of shopping for food is taken seriously in Paris.*

It is important to savour not only Paris but also its inhabitants, apparently so stand-offish but in reality just self-assured and proud of living in the unique and undisputed capital of France. If on their faces we can discern the marks of their hard metropolitan life, at the same time we can read that aspiration to provincial serenity that certain quarters and certain sections of town still harbour. In contrast to other city-dwellers, Parisians adapt themselves to continual urban growth. They move about on mopeds and bicycles just right for getting through the traffic. The drivers, too, face the traffic jams with detached resignation, while the old people meet in the gardens of the Grand Palais where they can daydream over games of canasta accompanied by wines brought from home. They play boules and have afternoon snacks, remembering how only a few years before they and their city were younger. Throngs of young people head for the legendary Beaubourg, whose space-age structures are the background to the incessant merrymaking of a country fair, with candy-floss sellers and fire-eaters. This colossus houses everything: a library, a museum of modern art, an open-air circus and centres of industrial avant-garde design. Its aim is to make culture accessible to the general public.

At first glance, the Beaubourg looks like a refinery, a rational piece of madness where the architects – the Italian Renzo Piani and the Englishman Richard Rogers – designed all the service systems along visual lines, everything clearly identifiable in different colours: red for the lifts, green for the water pipes, blue for the air-conditioning ducts, yellow for the electrical

45 The "Mouffe" or Rue Mouffetard, is one of Paris's oldest and busiest streets.

46 In the Marché aux Puces (Flea Market), more than 2000 stalls offer antiques, curios, clothes and all kinds of second-hand goods.

47 Inside the Luxembourg Gardens one can hire wooden boats to sail in the pools of the fountains.

48-49 Some parts of Paris are incredibly quiet: for example – the banks of the St. Martin Canal, the Jardins des Tuileries, or the Jardins des Plantes (Botanical Gardens).

50 Young visitors looking out on to the Rue Faubourg St. Honoré.

51 One can take a boat trip on the St. Martin Canal from Port de l'Arsenal to Bassine de la Villette, passing through several locks.

52-53 The Luxembourg Gardens contain many statues and splendid marble groups, including the Medici Fountain.

installations. The visual effects become bizarre, set against the deep electric blue of the Paris sky, always ready to involve you in one of its characteristic weather changes or in the existential wind so often evoked by Jean Paul Sartre.

Crowds of street performers gather in front of this museum and, against a backdrop of creative and architectural extravagance, they generate an atmosphere much like that of a mediaeval court. It is no mere chance that the Parisians themselves even more than the tourists gather here to admire their future and the greatest stimulation the city can offer. For every need Paris has an adequate answer, for every desire a suggestion, for every age congenial situations and surroundings which keep the difficulties inherent in life at as great a distance as possible.

Every Parisian is conscious of having been very important in the past and sure of being equally important in what is to come. In the slightly superior glance of these special Frenchmen we can read self-sufficiency, the assuredness of those who are content to live where they do even if it involves some sacrifices. The Parisians love their city because they have no doubts about the favours that it bestows every day, at every change of season and weather. Theirs is no closet love affair, however. They love without condition and almost always they are rewarded by a humanity that has never lessened, by the ancient insignia that flutter in the breeze, by the elegance of the women who grace the boulevards and by the tepid sun that warms the onlookers in the cafés.

8
8 F 30
LHEURE

GFD
OPTIONS S.A.

EMPLACEMENT
RÉSERVÉ
EXCLUSIVEMENT AUX
MÈRES DE FAMILLE
ET AUX ENFANTS

HOTEL VENDÔME
MORABITO

LA
PATACHE
EAUTOBUS

54 The Garden of the Palais Royal is entirely surrounded by splendid arcades.

55 Parc Monceau is one of the city's green oases. It was commissioned by the Duke of Orleans in the 18th century.

56 The Grand Cascade, an exclusive rendez-vous in the Bois de Boulogne is a good example of art nouveau style.

57 Moments of peace in the Jardin des Plantes where the oldest tree in Paris – a false acacia over 300 years old – can be found.

LA GRANDE CASCADE

58 *The colourful awnings over the balconies of the old buildings are typically Parisian.*

59 *The entrance to the Métro at Palais Royal is a wonderful piece of art nouveau ironwork.*

In Paris you have no difficulty in finding the space and the place to relax: you can cross the little market in Avenue de Saxe or stop for a brief snack at the Tuileries Gardens, or then again reorganize your thoughts on one of the many benches on the banks of the Seine. Paris truly offers an infinity of genuinely tranquil and picturesque oases. You will no doubt want to see the better-known things on the tourist circuit, but to ignore "les coins", the corners and the evocative hidden places of the city is to commit a grave error. By so doing you disregard the complexity of a great world composed of many fragments of life and humanity. Those who go in search of this intimate world of feelings and details must train the eye and the imagination. Above all it requires attention, a mental state of readiness in following the graceful, art nouveau lines of lamp posts and gates, the spaces and the play of light created by the juxtaposition of architectural styles. Paris possesses that rare capacity to surprise, thanks to a perennial alternation between the antique and the modern, between the quiet and the chaotic. The bizarre contrast between the slow glide of provincial life and cosmopolitan confusion amazes. In the same way an oasis of peace and silence in the midst of the clamour of the city should not cause surprise, it is thus that we find the St Martin Canal with its nine locks, numerous curving bridges and trees overhanging the water. The town-planners, disciples of the modern, would have liked to cage it, cement it, cover over this flow of water, but fortunately the plan was abandoned, thus guaranteeing the integrity of one of the most exquisitely romantic areas of Paris. Once again, this great capital has been saved from the need for space, and has shown a sort of innate wisdom in preserving itself – at least in part – from the mistakes and from the ruin which, albeit often dictated by concrete and urgent needs, has been inflicted on other great modern cities. So it is that we can continue to walk in a perennially young Latin Quarter, where the students go to buy books and note-pads of thin paper on which it is so pleasurable to write. Here we breathe an even fresher air near the 18th-century fountain built by Davioud and further on we can squeeze into the backstreets of the Saint Severin quartier, a remnant of mediaeval times lined with Greek and Arab delicatessens with a smoky air and cinemas that have escaped any restoration. Another jewel that has miraculously escaped the assault of the speculators is the Marais, to the north of the two Seine islands. It is this very Marais which boasts some of the most important Renaissance buildings in Europe, today put to use as museums or libraries. Here is an entire district that bears witness to the development of Paris from the reign of the brilliant Henry IV around the end of the 16th century up to the revolutionary and Jacobin surge. Houses and squares run into each other in perfect harmony, all in red brick and emanating a balanced charm. One of the most amusing and suitable ways to understand Paris is to stroll aimlessly through the Marais, between the shops, the little bistros, the cafés, and the courtyards of the most beautiful town houses. Or you could discover the provinciality of Paris in Montmartre which is a myth that is regularly reborn without becoming tarnished. Always renowned as a centre of artistic and bohemian life, this area acts as a centre of attraction for

ME

60-61 An important part of Paris's charm is linked to the Seine, which divides the city in two, and flows around the Ile de Cité and the Ile Saint-Louis.

62-63 A "bateau-mouche" takes tourists on a voyage of discovery of Paris, and is probably the best way to start sight-seeing on a first visit.

64-65 Street theatre in front of the "Les Deux Magots" in St. Germain-des-Prés, one of the most lively areas of the city, and a meeting-place for intellectual night-birds.

many intellectual activities. A few steps further brings you to Place des Abbesses or Place Goudeau where Picasso invented cubism and Apollinaire composed his frenetic and surrealist verses. Van Gogh, Renoir, Utrillo, and Gauguin all lived and created in these streets. The facades in carved wood, the signs and the craft shops constitute a real and independent chapter among the marvels of Paris. Elements of baroque and art nouveau style blend in with lettering in red and gold. The classical and almost bare shop windows, decorated only by simple curtains and orderly shelves, take us back to the early 19th century to an art elsewhere devoured by consumerism and neon. It is not difficult to find this atmosphere in Rue du Faubourg Saint Honoré, in Avenue George Cinq, in the boulangeries scattered all around which offer the legendary loaves of French bread. Do not ask for paper or bags, for it is all part of an ancient rite. Do not believe you could or should change it. Another extraordinary peculiarity of Paris is its cemeteries. The one in Montmartre, like the more famous Père-Lachaise, offers an atmosphere which is anything but sad: if anything, it is pensive. These places, it is as well to emphasise, are not at all depressing and are like places of pilgrimage for citizens and tourists alike. Lying here side by side are the heroes of the Commune and celebrated writers or artists like Alfred de Musset, Modigliani, Rossini, Bellini, Chopin, La Fontaine, Molière, Bizet, Isadora Duncan, Oscar Wilde, Gertrude Stein, Proust and Balzac.

Aux Deux Mag
CAFE DE FLORE

Aux

66-67 Place du Tertre, frequented by artists and intellectuals, manages to preseve a delightful provincial atmosphere. The square, always full of artists and tourists, was at one time the heart of the old village of Montmartre.

chez EUGENE
TARIF TERRASSE
SNACK
POULET

68 The Basilica of Sacré-Coeur, a strange mixture of Byzantine, late Gothic, Classical and other styles. Built entirely from the white stone of Château-Loudon, it was erected as a symbol of penitence after the French defeat in the Franco-Prussian War of 1870.

69 Place du Tertre, with its artists and typical restaurants, is one of the most important tourist attractions of the city.

70 A viewing platform on the Beaubourg or Centre Georges Pompidou by the architects Renzo Piano and Richard Rogers. Inside can be found the Musée National d'Art Moderne, the Centre de Création Industrielle, the Bibliotèque Publique d'Information, the Institut de Recherche et de Coordination Acoustique et Musical.

71 The futuristic structure of the Beaubourg: the centre was created to bring culture closer to Parisians and tourists, and has become one of the most important symbols of modern Paris.

72-73 One of the gargoyles of Notre-Dame scans the skyline, which includes the "boiler-house" architecture of the Beaubourg.

74-75 Metallic structures and space-age elevators on the exterior of the building take visitors high up above the roofs of Paris.

76-77 Built during the reign of Napoleon III, the iron buildings of the old Halles were for a long time a picturesque market site. Demolished in 1971, they have been replaced by a modern cultural and commercial centre: the Forum des Halles.

LE FRONT NATIONAL
DE LIBERATION DU
KURDISTAN

BRAS DE FIER
CHRISTOPHE MALAVOY
Restaurant
Jacques
Pergay

Croque-Gourmand

78 The complex of La Défense, a high-rise town on the outskirts of Paris, was built in little more than 25 years starting in 1956. For its design, several of the most important architects in the world took part and the most modern construction techniques were used.

79 One of the buildings in La Défense. The complex is divided into the "Quartier d'Affaires" and the "Quartier du Parc" inside which can be found a theatre and a botanic garden containing 900 different species of plants.

80-81 La Défense, the Manhattan of Paris, contains many examples of futuristic architecture. It is also a centre for international exhibitions.

82-83 The Palais de Justice (Law Courts), for centuries the seat of the civil and judicial system, forms part of a large complex which includes the Sainte-Chapelle and the Conciergerie.

fnac
LES FORUMS DE LA COMMUNICATION
DECEMBRE 89
Infomart
Congrès-Expositions

84 Fireworks at the Eiffel Tower: the celebration of the bicentenary of the Revolution. The Tower was erected in 1887-1889. Two hundred million visitors have walked around its platforms. An entire day can be spent there, shopping, dining, and admiring the splendid view of the city.

85 The Eiffel Tower and the Trocadéro Fountain at night.

86-87 Paris by night is a legend. Immortalized in the paintings of Toulouse-Lautrec, Parisian nightlife has lost none of its vigour over the years. The Moulin Rouge, the Folies Bergères, and Crazy Horse Saloon continue to exert an incredible attraction.

MOULIN ROUGE
DU
Wembacher

Hamburger
TABAC
Hamburger

88 Situated on the Left Bank of the Seine, the Quartier Latin is one of the most lively areas of the entire city.

89 Aerial view from the Eiffel Tower; the Place du Trocadéro and the Palais de Chaillot can be seen and, in the background, the skyscrapers of La Défense.

Paris is a city of bitter-sweet contrasts, where the frenzy of modern life is softened by the atmosphere of the often soft, never blinding, light. Few cities in the world have shown that Parisian ability to make such a sagacious use of daylight and to create such special night effects with lighting. Every single view, every monument, from Notre-Dame, to the Seine, or the Beaubourg, takes on a special tone with each hour that passes. Thus the buildings in Place des Vosges and the towers of steel and glass of the Défense appear fascinatingly different in the light of day. If the 17th-century mansions seem to placidly absorb the rays of the sun, the skyscrapers aggressively reflect them as if to bring to mind the hardness of the world they represent.
At nightfall a whole new world awakes and shows itself, assuming mysterious and captivating guises. In the brief spell that separates sunset from total obscurity, everything changes rapidly to weave more magic spells. It is above all the old stone that benefits from the progress of the night; marble spires and obelisks now launch themselves in a more solitary manner into the sky; ephemeral shadows are born and new perspectives lengthen, sometimes threatening and sometimes curiously strange.
Notre-Dame, with its fabulous mediaeval gargoyles, seems to lean over the city as if to lay claim to its primacy and its desire to squash the pilgrim with its majesty. The obelisk in Place Vendôme, throwing off the garb of traffic roundabout, rises up among lamp-posts and palaces, proud of its regality. And it is these same tricks of light that give the Eiffel Tower a new vitality. The gigantic network of metal is again as surprising as in its first years when it provoked amazement mixed with intolerance: even the Champs Elysées finds a grand self-celebration in the perspectives created by the shadows of night. Entire quarters see an incredible character change in the course of 24 hours: such is the case of the middle-class quarter of Pigalle, by day crossed by clerks and quiet routine-bound families, by night an intense and sometimes ambiguous world, characterised by pulsating neon lights, smoky beer-houses, individuals on the edges of legality, visitors in search of the forbidden. Naturally, the Paris night does not only offer shadows and easy pick-ups. On the streets there is a certain gaiety, the citizens enjoy meeting each other, especially the younger ones who throng the steps of the Sacré-Coeur. The lights wink and shine in the cafés, and those of Montparnasse are by far the friendliest: the Closerie des Lilas, which before the Great War was the meeting place for Lenin and Trotsky, the famous Select open all night, the Dome and the Rotonde, all overlook the Boulevard de Montparnasse.
The splendour of Paris night-life finds its highest and most intense point during the celebrations for the anniversary of the storming of the Bastille. On the night between the 14 and 15 July the capital's sky becomes the ideal theatre for fantastic displays of fireworks which explode, lighting up the flag-bedecked city, which seems to have gone crazy. Everybody goes down into the street and celebrates the great revolutionary Utopia. This festive cheerfulness mingles with the innate class of the people and the city.
Certainly it is no mere chance that Paris has been named "Ville

90-91 Built for the World Fair of 1889, the Eiffel Tower represents even today, an extraordinary technical achievement. For its construction 15,000 pieces of metal were used together with 2,500,000 rivets. At 984 feet, it was the tallest construction in the world at that time.

Lumière" – the city of light . . . And yet, when all is said and done, even this name, like all the others which have attempted to define this city in a single formula, is not sufficient. Despite the problems of the nuclear age, Paris has kept its magical atmosphere magic, a centuries-old charm which not even the continuous assault of millions of tourists can lessen; it will always remain an elegant, exclusive and aristocratic European city that lends itself with poise and balance to urban sprawl, keeping hidden corners and virtues known only to certain Parisians who keep its secrets. It is an instinctive city and it is thus that it should be experienced, without too much rationality. "For Paris there will be no end and the memories of those who have lived there all differ from person to person", explains Hemingway. Everybody should look for his own Paris, forgetting all that he has seen or heard, or better still, putting it into a corner of the mind to be brought out later and compared with the infinite aspects of a single complex reality.

92 It is to easy to see why Paris has been called "city of light": this picture shows the Arc de Triomphe magnificently flood-lit.

93 To celebrate the 14th of July (Bastille Day), the entire city is transformed: from the Arc de Triomphe rays of light representing the colours of the French flag are projected into the sky.

94-95 The delicate evening light make this stretch of the Seine near Neuilly even more beautiful.

J'ai laissé mon
à PARIS